MILLBROOK ARTS LIBRARY

PEOPLE IN ART

by Anthea Peppin

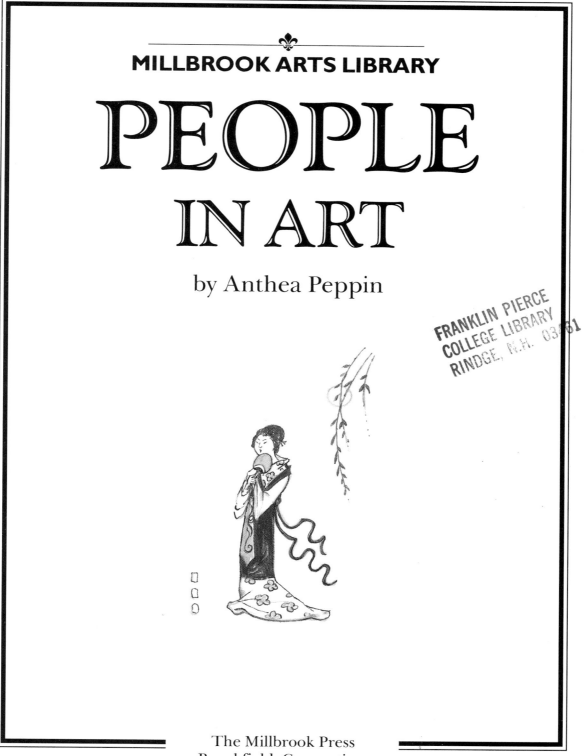

The Millbrook Press
Brookfield, Connecticut

Copyright © 1991 Merlion Publishing Ltd
First published in the United States in 1992 by
The Millbrook Press Inc.
2 Old New Milford Road
Brookfield, Connecticut 06804

Design: Paul Fielder
Series Editor: Charlotte Ryrie

Printed in Spain by Cronion SA

Library of Congress Cataloging-in-Publication Data

Peppin, Anthea
    People in art / Anthea Peppin.
      p. cm. – – (Millbrook arts library)
    Includes index.
    Summary: Examines the ways that people are depicted in various
kinds of art and describes some of the techniques used.
    ISBN 1-56294-171-2
    1. Humans in art – – Juvenile literature. 2. Visual perception –
– Juvenile literature. [1. Humans in art. 2. Art – – Technique.
3. Art appreciation.] I. Title. II. Title: People in art.
III. Series: Peppin, Anthea. Millbrook arts library.
N7625.5.P46 1992
704.9'42 – – dc20   91-34983
                                                  CIP
                                                  AC

Cover artwork by Richard Berridge and Gwen and Shirley Tourret
(B L Kearley Ltd); photography by Mike Stannard.

Artwork on pages 9, 17 by Tim Beer; pages 4, 11, 15, 20, 23, 24-25,
26-27, 34, 37, 39, 43 by Paul Fielder; pages 6, 13 by Mike
Lacey; page 19 by Jeremy Plumb and page 41 by Helen Williams.

Photographs on pages 4, 11, 15, 19, 20, 23, 24-25, 28-29, 34, 37,
39, 42-43 by Mike Stannard.

CONTENTS

All kinds of lines

A quick way to make a picture is with lines. When you look at something such as a chair or a table, you imagine there is a line around it. The line isn't really there — your eyes invent it, to separate the object you are looking at from its background. When you want to make a drawing, it is this imaginary line that you put on your paper. The line shows the shape of the object you are looking at. It is called an outline.

Learning about lines

You can make many different kinds of line — thin, thick, light, dark, smooth, straight, curved. Use a pencil, a crayon, and a felt-tip pen to draw lines on a sheet of paper. Look at the differences in the lines.

This cave painting of hunters or warriors was found at Valltorta, in Spain.

Thick and thin lines

Long ago, cave people covered the walls of their caves with pictures of people and animals. They painted them with large, thick lines. These were probably made with sharpened sticks dipped in colored earth. The people they painted look strong and bold.

This picture is by the Italian artist Raphael. It was drawn nearly 500 years ago. He has drawn a young man with black chalk, using many different kinds of line. There is a strong outline around the face and hat. But the hair has been drawn with thin strokes to show that it is fine and soft.

Make a drawing of the palm of your hand. Begin with the outline. Then take a pencil with a fine point and fill in as many lines as you can.

Portrait of a Young Man was drawn by the Italian artist Raphael.

Now try drawing someone's hair, or the folds in their clothes. Keep your collection of line drawings together. You may want to look back at them as you read the next part of the book.

A portrait of yourself

A portrait is a picture of a person. Artists often paint their own portraits as well as those of other people. A portrait of yourself is called a self-portrait.

Try drawing your self-portrait. You will need a mirror, some paper, and a pencil. Sit at a table and prop up the mirror so that you can see yourself easily. Now you can begin to draw your face. First, sketch the positions of your eyes, nose, and mouth. Look carefully at your head — notice that your eyes are about

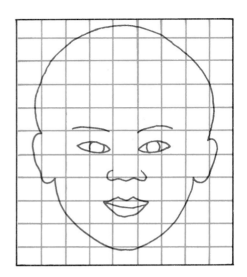

halfway down. How much room does your nose take up? How far is your mouth from your nose?

Shade in the shadows

A real face has bumps and hollows. But the picture you are drawing is flat. How do you make your flat picture look more lifelike? Look at this self-portrait by the German artist Albrecht Dürer. He has made his face appear solid by shading in the parts that are in shadow. If you look at your own face in the mirror, you will see that some areas are darker than others. Shade in these areas on your picture, using your pencil. Soon your picture will stop looking flat and start to look like a real face.

The German artist Albrecht Dürer painted this self-portrait when he was only 13.

Portrait of an artist

Rembrandt van Rijn was a famous Dutch artist who lived in the 1600s. He was very popular and painted many portraits of wealthy people. All his life he was his own favorite model, and he painted about 70 self-portraits. The earlier ones show him looking very successful and pleased with life. This one was painted shortly before he died, when he was old and quite poor.

This was the last self-portrait painted by the Dutch artist Rembrandt van Rijn.

Light and dark

The Orrery was painted by the English artist Joseph Wright.

Many artists look at the effects of light and dark in their paintings. People can look strange and unfamiliar if their faces are in shadow, or if they are lit up by a bright light.

Look at this painting by the English artist Joseph Wright. It shows some people looking at an orrery, which is a clockwork model that shows the movements of the planets around the sun. There is a bright light in the center of the picture that comes from the model sun. Can you see how it lights up the children's faces? Notice the interesting shadows on the clothes and faces of the other figures.

Paint yourself in shadow

Try painting your face in this dramatic way. You will need a flashlight, a mirror, some paper, paints, brushes, a pencil, and a palette. Stand in front of the mirror in a dark room. Shine the flashlight onto your face from above, from below, and from the side. See how different you look! Then prop up the flashlight so that your hands are free. Begin your picture by sketching in the outlines of your face with a pencil. To paint your face, first mix your skin color.

Add small amounts of white paint to your skin color to paint places where your face is lit by the flashlight, and black where it is in shadow. Some shadows contain blue or purple tints also.

What is form?

You are a solid object. So is a table, a chair, or a tree. You are not flat, like a piece of paper. You have form.

We can understand form more easily through touch. Ask some friends to help you with an experiment. First, put some small objects from around your home into a box.

Ask your friends to close their eyes and take turns in picking out an object from the box. How much can they tell you about each form just by turning it around in their hands?

Walk around a sculpture

A sculptor is an artist who enjoys making solid forms, rather than flat paintings. These are called sculptures. This large sculpture was carved from stone by the British sculptor Henry Moore. You can see only part of the sculpture from looking at this photograph. You really need to walk around it and look at it from several different positions.

This sculpture by Henry Moore is called *Recumbent Figure* — a person lying down.

This is a sculpture
of an Inuit mother
and her child.

All kinds of sculpture

Sculptures can be all shapes and sizes.
They can be larger than a house, or
small enough to stand on a table. You
can make a sculpture from almost
anything. An Inuit carved this small
sculpture from a soft, heavy stone called
soapstone. Can you imagine how it
would feel to touch? You can explore
sculptures with your fingertips as well as
with your eyes.

Make your own sculpture

Most stone is too hard to work on
without special tools. If you want to try
making a sculpture, begin with a soft
material such as soap. Find a block of
soap, then cover a table with newspaper.
Ask which knife you may use, and
remember to be careful — if it's sharp
enough to cut the soap, it may also
cut you!

Try carving a face or a figure. Keep
turning the form around in your hands
to see how it changes from all sides.
When you are pleased with your
sculpture, brush off any scrapings of
soap and put it somewhere dry.

Shapes in silhouette

If we draw a simple outline of an object and then color it black, we make a silhouette. This shows us the shape of the object.

In Europe during the 1700s, silhouette portraits became popular. The portrait were either painted black or cut out from black paper and put on a white background. They usually showed the profile, or side view, of a person's head. A clever artist could get a good likeness of a person. Sometimes he might even show whole groups of people this way.

The word *silhouette* comes from the name of a French politician Étienne de Silhouette who lived in the 1700s. He was famous for being very stingy. His name became used for things that could be made very cheaply. It was much cheaper to have a silhouette portrait made than to have a portrait painted

This is a silhouette of a man cutting his own silhouette.

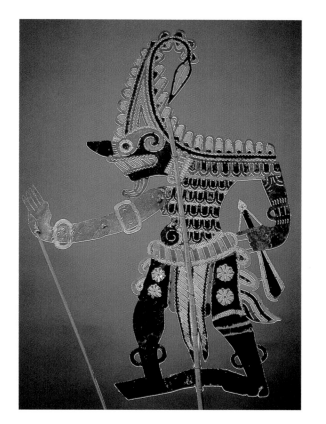

These two shadow puppets come from Malaysia.

Shadow stories

We can also make silhouettes with shadows. In some countries, special shadow puppets are used to perform plays. In Malaysia, shadow puppets like these are finely carved and decorated. Each puppet has moving joints. Sticks are attached to the back so that the puppets can be operated by hand. A screen is placed in front of the puppets. A light shines behind them to cast a shadow on the screen. The audience sits in front of the screen and watches the silhouettes of the puppets.

A silhouette portrait

Try to make a silhouette portrait of someone you know. First draw his or her profile. Then you can either paint it black or cut it from black paper with scissors. You could use the same technique as the Malaysian puppeteers to help you. Make a screen by hanging up a large piece of white paper or cloth. Place the person you want to copy behind it. Make sure the person is sitting sideways. Then shine a light behind so that a shadow of the person's profile appears on the screen. This makes a silhouette for you to copy.

Asian brushstrokes

The Hunt is a book illustration by the Japanese artist Masayoshi.

A Japanese artist named Masayoshi painted these pictures about 200 years ago. They were painted to illustrate stories in a book. There are lots of people, all busy doing different things. If you look carefully, you can also see that each figure is drawn using only two or three separate lines.

Masayoshi used a brush with a fine point. He painted in long strokes without taking his brush off the paper. In some places the lines are thin, but in other places the figures look solid. The thick lines are made by leaning the brush against the paper, and the thin lines are made by drawing with the tip.

This style is good for showing movement, and figures really look full of energy. Can you draw in this lively way?

Your own brush drawing

Drawing with a brush can be very difficult. Choose a soft one with a point, or use a special brush pen. First practice making different kinds of stroke. Try making straight and curved lines. Make them thick and thin without taking your brush off the paper. When you feel confident, choose what you are going to draw. See if you can draw a figure using less than six separate strokes.

You can use a pencil instead of a brush, but it must have a broad lead so that you can make thick and thin lines. It is quite difficult to show movement using pencil lines in this way, unless you are already very skillful.

People from ancient Egypt

Hunting Fowl in the Marshes was painted on the wall of the tomb of Nebamun, in Thebes.

Ancient Egyptian artists had an interesting way of painting people. Let's look carefully at this picture. It shows a man named Nebamun, who is hunting birds in the marshes. Notice that we see his head from the side, but his eye is painted as if we are looking at it from the front. Nebamun's legs and feet are shown sideways, too, but his arms and shoulders are turned to face us. Try standing in this position. It's not very comfortable!

Painting things clearly

Why do you think the ancient Egyptian artists painted people in this strange way? They thought it was important to show images clearly, even if the paintings didn't look absolutely true to life. So they did not paint exactly what they saw, but painted things in the way that seemed most clear to them.

There are other unusual things in this picture. Can you see Nebamun's wife and daughter? The artist has painted them much smaller than Nebamun, to show that he thinks they are less important. There are also many different birds in the picture. How many can you count? Do you think you would see so many different kinds at one time?

An ancient Egyptian family

Try drawing or painting your own family in this style. You don't have to copy them from real life, but draw them from memory as the ancient Egyptians did. Use bright colors and include as many details as you can. Whom do you draw the largest? Are they the most important people in your family?

What is a caricature?

King Louis Philippe Turning into a Pear in 4 Stages was drawn by the French artist Honoré Daumier.

Have you seen cartoons in newspapers? They often show famous people, such as politicians or movie stars. They are often drawn in an unkind way that exaggerates certain things about them. This type of drawing is called a caricature.

Caricatures are meant to make fun of the people they show. An artist chooses certain features about a person, such as their nose or their teeth, then draws these features in an exaggerated way. If the person is famous for doing something in particular, such as talking too much, the caricature may exaggerate that activity, too.

Here is a well-known French caricature drawn about 150 years ago. It shows a French king turning into a pear. In France at that time it was very rude to call somebody a pear because it meant they were stupid. The artist is making fun of the king, whose name was Louis Philippe, for eating too much. The artist was also suggesting the king was a fool.

Drawing your own caricature

Try drawing your own caricature. Choose a friend who likes to have fun. Ask yourself what is special about him or her. Are they tall and skinny? Do their ears stick out? Do they have a funny hairstyle? Do they smile a lot? Perhaps there is something they particularly like doing, such as bicycling or reading books. When you have decided what to exaggerate, draw your caricature in pencil. The best caricatures are drawn in a very sketchy way without much detail, so try not to put too many lines in your picture. Does the finished picture make you laugh? Does it make your friend laugh, too?

Fantastic faces

Have you ever seen a face made from plants before? An Italian artist named Giuseppe Arcimboldo, who lived in the 1500s, liked to paint faces made up of plants.

If you look at this painting from far away it just looks like an ordinary picture of a strange man. But when you look more closely, you can see that the man is made up of different plants. Can you recognize many of the different fruits, flowers, and vegetables? Notice that each plant has been painted with great care. The pear that makes the man's nose looks so real that you almost want to pick it up and eat it!

A plant portrait

Arcimboldo spent a long time painting the plants in his pictures so that they looked really lifelike. You can create a similar effect by using cutout photographs from magazines.

You will need a pile of old magazines, a large sheet of paper, some scissors, and glue. First, search through the magazines for photographs of fruit, flowers, and vegetables. Carefully cut out the ones that you want to use. Decide whether your portrait is going to be a side view or a front view. Then choose some of your photographs and arrange them on the paper in the shape of a face. When you are happy with the result, glue the photographs to the paper.

Vertumnus was painted by the Italian artist Giuseppe Arcimboldo for the Hapsburg emperor, Rudolf.

African masks

The masks on this page come from Africa. They were made to wear on special occasions, or ceremonies. Each ceremony celebrates a particular time of year, or marks a special event, such as a wedding or a funeral. There is usually dancing and music, and bright costumes are worn. The dances often tell stories about a tribe's history. Different tribes have always had different styles of mask and decoration.

Many African tribes are very talented at wood carving. This mask of a hyena's head is carefully carved. Other masks may be decorated with paint or feathers. Some masks were meant to make people laugh. Others were sad, or frightening. How does this decorated mask make you feel?

This is a ritual mask from the Yoruba tribe.

An Ibo tribesman carved this hyena's head mask.

This decorated mask from the Ivory Coast was made 100 years ago.

Making your own mask

You can easily make your own mask from cardboard. You will also need some paint and a collection of other materials for decoration. You might like to add feathers, buttons, leaves, or scraps of cloth. Use whatever you can find! First decide what shape you want the mask to be and cut it out.

Then make your eyeholes. Round eyeholes can make your mask look surprised. Eyeholes that slant downward can make it look sad. Holes slanting upward can seem angry. Try different shapes on a piece of paper before you mark them on the cardboard and cut them out. You can cut out holes for your mouth and your nose, or you can paint them. You can even glue on different things to make a mouth and nose.

It is fun sticking lots of different materials on your mask to make it interesting. But make sure that all the glue is dry before you start to paint. African masks are often painted in vivid patterns. Your mask can also look powerful if you use just one bold color.

Let's look at color

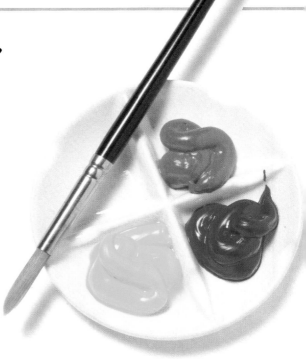

The world is full of colors — they are everywhere we look. Most artists are interested in using color. They can make almost any color they wish by mixing together their paints.

The three primary colors

Red, blue, and yellow are called primary colors. This means that we can't make them by mixing together any other colors.

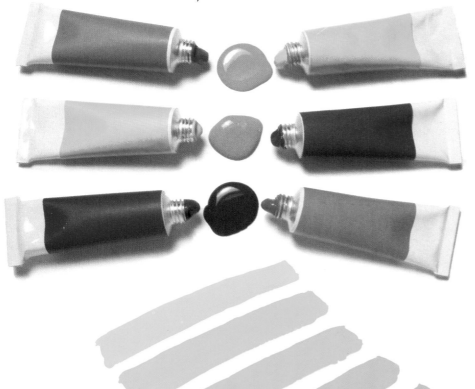

But if we mix primary colors together we can make many, many more colors! For example, when we mix red and yellow paint together, we make orange. But we don't always make the same color orange.

Mixing colors

Put some yellow paint on your palette and add a tiny amount of red paint to the yellow. Mix them together with a little water. With a clean brush, paint a stripe of the color you have made near the edge of your paper. Now mix a little more red into the paint on your palette. Paint a stripe of this new color next to the first. Continue adding red and painting stripes. You'll see that red and yellow can make many different colors — from a golden yellow to an orangey red.

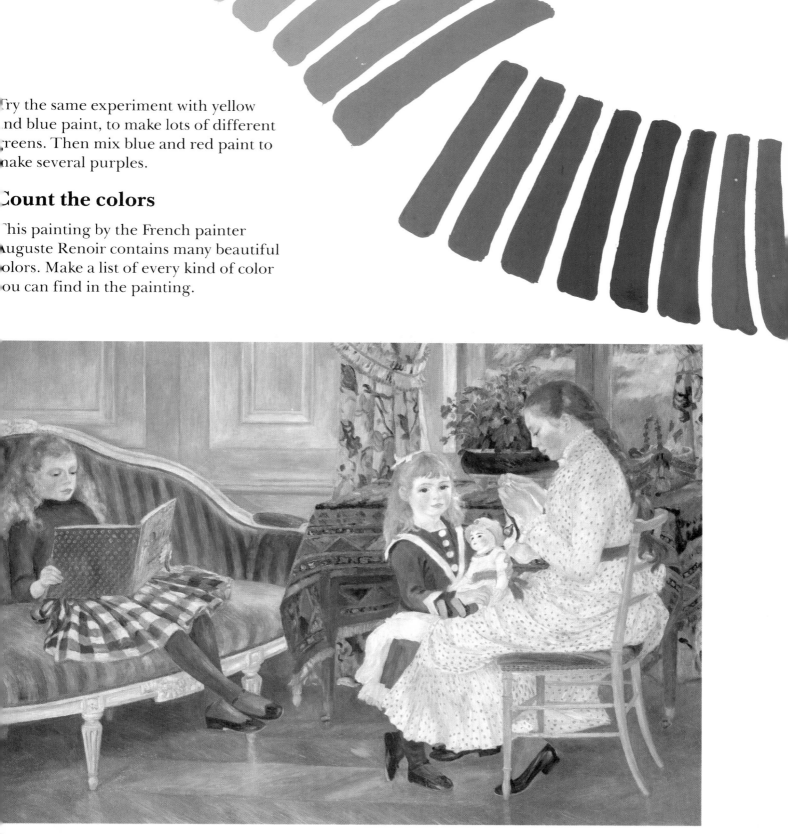

Try the same experiment with yellow and blue paint, to make lots of different greens. Then mix blue and red paint to make several purples.

Count the colors

This painting by the French painter Auguste Renoir contains many beautiful colors. Make a list of every kind of color you can find in the painting.

The Children's Afternoon at Wargemont was painted by the French painter Auguste Renoir.

Color mixing

The primary colors — red, blue, and yellow — cannot be made by mixing other colors together. The secondary colors — green, orange, and purple — are made by mixing two primary colors. Blue and yellow mixed together make green. Red and yellow make orange. Red and blue make purple.

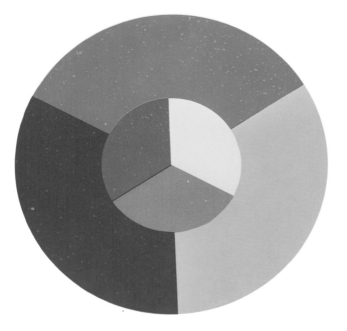

Complementary colors are like opposite colors. They stand out from each other and do not blend together. Red and green are complementary. Yellow and purple are complementary, as are blue and orange. Look at the color wheel. It will help you to see which colors are primary, secondary, and complementary.

Using tiny colored dots

This painting is by the French painter Georges Seurat. He tried different ways of mixing colors. Instead of mixing

them before he painted, he used tiny dots of primary colors next to each other. He painted green grass by using blue and yellow dots together.

Sunday Afternoon on the Island of La Grande Jatte was painted by the French artist Georges Seurat.

ometimes he put in a few dots of omplementary color as well. He put a ew dots of red in the grass because he hought it would make the green stand ut more. You can see this clearly in the magnified picture.

ry using colored dots for yourself. aint some red and blue dots together. Iow far away do you have to stand for

them to look purple? The smaller you make the dots, the nearer you will be able to stand.

Color your mood!

A Maid Combing a Woman's Hair was painted by the French artist Edgar Degas.

Color is powerful! Looking at colors can make you feel happy, sad, calm, or excited. In other words, colors can change your mood.

Most artists think of reds and yellows as warm colors. This may be because they are the colors of fire or the sun — which are both hot! In this painting by Edgar Degas, a woman is leaning back in her chair while another woman brushes her long hair. The artist has used mainly reds and oranges. Perhaps he wanted us to feel that the room is warm and the woman is relaxed.

Changing tones

Painters can change the mood of a painting by making the colors lighter or darker. This is called changing the tone. We use black and white to change the tone of primary colors.

Put some red paint on your palette. Paint a stripe of red near the edge of your paper. Now add a tiny spot of black paint to your red. Paint a stripe of the new color next to the old one.

Continue painting more stripes, adding a little more black each time. As you add black, the color becomes richer and darker. You might want to use deep colors such as these to paint a nighttime scene.

Bright, sunny yellows

Wash your brush and experiment with yellow paint. This time, add white a little at a time. The strong yellow will become lighter and clearer in tone. These yellow colors can give a painting a feeling of sunshine.

Dull, sad blues

Now mix up some gray paint. Start with white and add black a little at a time, until you get gray. Then put some blue paint on another part of your palette. Paint a stripe of blue on your paper. Now add a small amount of gray to the blue. Paint some stripes as you did before, mixing in a little more gray each time.

Adding gray makes colors lose their brightness and become dull. You can use dull tones like these to paint a cold, rainy day. Dull colors give a painting a sad mood.

Paint your mood

Artists have to decide on the mood of a picture before they begin to paint. Then they choose tones to match that feeling. You can make a mood picture of your own. Think of things that make you happy and excited, angry and upset, or sad. You don't have to paint a scene. Just use color to show your feeling.

The Scream was painted by the Norwegian artist Edvard Munch.

Colors and feelings

A man stands at the edge of a bridge. His hands are clasped to his head. His eyes are huge and staring, and his mouth is opened wide to scream. His face is crooked and twisted. Behind him, the landscape is a swirling mass of bright lines, and the clouds are the color of blood. There are two other figures at the far end of the bridge. They are thin and dark.

The picture is called *The Scream*. It was painted by the Norwegian artist Edvard Munch. Everything in the picture expresses chaos. The colors of the scenery are bold and not what we would expect. They seem to be copying the distress of the screaming man. The colors shock us. They make us feel disturbed.

Frightening colors

Munch is not simply trying to paint some figures in a landscape. He is using shapes and colors to express a deep feeling. His painting expresses fear. Something terrible has happened, but we do not know what it is. Munch was one of several artists who became known as Expressionists. They felt strongly that paintings could show people worrying and suffering, as well as showing the beautiful things in life.

A happy feeling

A completely different feeling is being shown in the other picture. The French painter Paul Gauguin was living on the Pacific island of Tahiti. He painted many pictures of the people there. The climate is hot, and the days are very bright. These women look happy to be sitting chatting lazily in the sun. The strong, simple colors make us feel happy and contented.

Gauguin's own life was actually very unhappy. We could never guess this from looking at his paintings.

Tahitian Women on the Beach was painted by the French artist Paul Gauguin.

Individual portraits

When somebody has their portrait painted, they like to be made to look their best. Kings and queens and rulers are usually painted to look very important. They may be wearing their grandest robes and jewels, or dressed in a smart uniform. Perhaps they will be standing in a splendid room, or have part of a grand building in the background. A portrait does not usually show somebody wearing ordinary clothes or looking plain, even if this is how they really look in everyday life.

A flattering picture

Here is a picture of Henrietta Maria, the wife of Charles I, a king who ruled England in the 1600s. She looks very attractive in this painting. Somebody who knew her said that the queen was actually very small with skinny arms and huge teeth that stuck out! The artist who painted this picture was asked to paint the queen many more times. She was obviously pleased that he made her look much more beautiful than she was.

Portrait of Henrietta Maria was painted by the Flemish artist Anthony van Dyck.

Girl in a Red Dress
was painted by
the American artist
Ammi Phillips.

Portraits of ordinary people

Ordinary people can be made to look beautiful or important, also. Look at this picture of an ordinary Japanese girl. The artist has shown her wearing flowing clothes that fall gracefully around her. The colors are very delicate. The flower behind the girl is also very graceful and delicate. The combination of shapes and colors makes us think the girl is very beautiful.

The little American girl in the picture looks pretty in her best clothes. She has her favorite animal with her. She looks serious. Perhaps she is trying very hard to sit still!

Your own portrait

If you wanted to have your portrait painted, how would you like to look? Would you like to look very grand, or very beautiful? Perhaps you would like to look very clever, or very rich. Think about what clothes you would wear, and what other details you would like to see included.

Woman and Chrysanthemums is a color woodcut by the Japanese artist Utagawa Kuniyoshi.

Miniature pictures

This tiny portrait, *Girl with Apple*, was painted by the English artist Isaac Oliver.

Do you have a picture of someone who is special to you? If you do, it's probably a photograph. Long ago, before cameras were invented, people sometimes treasured tiny paintings. Some of them were so small that they could fit into the palm of your hand. Sometimes people attached them to gold chains to hang around their necks.

English miniature portraits

These tiny English portraits were painted about 400 years ago. They were painted on vellum, which is fine calf's skin. The paintings are the same size as they are shown here. The little girl is dressed in her best clothes. The picture has been enlarged to show you the beautifully painted lace on her collar, and the pattern on her dress. The artist must have used a brush with only one or two hairs to paint such fine detail.

A handsome young man

Perhaps this picture of a smart young Englishman was a present for his lover. He looks very romantic leaning against the rose tree. You can tell from his fine clothes that he was rich. These paintings usually show people from wealthy families. It was expensive to have a miniature portrait painted.

Persian miniatures

There is a picture of a Persian miniature painting on page 40 in this book. These pictures were made for wealthy rulers who kept them in a book, like an album. Persian artists used brushes made from fine hairs from kittens or squirrels when they painted these tiny pictures. They painted the colors in different layers, and even used gold to paint fine details on the top layer. It could take an artist sixty days to complete just one small painting.

Make your own miniature

Try drawing a miniature portrait of your favorite person. Mark a circle or oval on a piece of stiff white paper. It should not be more than 2 inches (5 centimeters) across. Use very sharp colored pencils, and work slowly and carefully. You will not get good results if you rush.

Miniature silhouettes were also popular in Europe 100 years ago. You can find out how to make a silhouette on page 12.

Portrait of a Young Man was painted by the English artist Nicholas Hilliard.

Giant figures

The Statue of Liberty stands outside New York.

Works of art can be enormous. When we think of art, we often think of pictures hung on walls, or objects in special galleries. In fact, many works of art can be seen in more everyday places.

The Statue of Liberty

The Statue of Liberty is a huge figure of a woman carrying a flaming torch. This figure stands in New York Harbor. It suggests that travelers are entering a country where freedom is important. The statue was actually made by a Frenchman just over 100 years ago. It was made from 300 different pieces, which were sent by boat from France to New York. It must have been a difficult job to put them all together!

A huge statue of Buddha

This giant Japanese figure of Buddha is 14 yards (13 meters) tall. Buddha was a prince who gave up all his riches. He then taught people a better way of life. These teachings became the foundations of Buddhism, one of the world's great religions.

Look around your local town. What different works of art can you see? Are they large or small? Think about how the images were made, and why they are there. What would you like to see?

The Great Buddha is at Kamokora, in Japan.

Make a life-size figure

You can make a large figure, too. You need a big piece of paper. You might be able to find an old roll of wallpaper, or join several small sheets of paper together. Ask a friend or a member of your family to lie down on the paper, and draw around them. Use a thick black pen. You will then have an outline to color in. Try to get the face to look as realistic as possible. You can paint the clothes with bright colors and interesting patterns. When you have finished the figure, cut it out. Does it look like a real person when you pin it on a wall?

Crowds of people

Children's Games was painted by the Flemish artist Pieter Brueghel the Elder.

There are many ways of painting crowds of people. Some artists paint each person in a crowd clearly. Other artists show only the details of the people in the front of the picture. This picture of crowds of children playing games is full of detail. The people in the distance look just as real as the ones in the front of the picture. The artist, Pieter Brueghel, painted in Flanders in the 1500s. You can learn a lot about life in a Flemish town at that time from looking at this picture. You can see the clothes people wore and the games they played. Do you recognize any of the games? Do you play any similar games?

Faces in the front row

Look at the other picture of a crowd. The Italian artist Duccio has painted it o you see only the faces of the front row. You know that there are other people behind them because you can ee the tops of their heads. When Duccio was painting in Italy, in the 400s, most pictures were painted to Illustrate stories about the Christian religion. Artists wanted to show the main characters in each story, but did not always think it was important to paint all the other people in such detail.

Make your own crowd picture

First you must plan your picture of a crowd. What sort of crowd do you want o show? How many people will there be? Will people be spaced out or packed losely together? You could choose people at a sports event, at school, or in a busy street. What sort of clothes will hey be wearing?

Then you need to decide on your iewing point. If you are looking traight at a crowd, you may see only the front row in detail. If you are looking down at a crowd, as if you are on a stage and they are the audience, you will be able to see what the people farthest away are doing. Draw the front row first. Do not forget that people in the distance will appear smaller than people in the front of your picture.

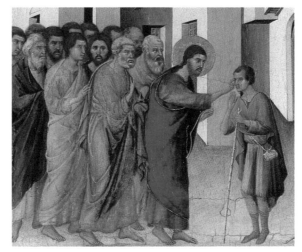

Jesus Opens the Eyes of a Man Born Blind was painted by the Italian artist Duccio di Buoninsegna.

Images from Islam

Muslims are people who follow the religion of Islam. They pray in a mosque where the walls are often richly decorated. These decorations include brightly colored patterns, pictures of flowers, and flowing Arabic writing. The floors of mosques are covered with carpets and rugs of bright colors and complicated designs.

There are no pictures showing people in mosques. But there are many beautiful and lifelike paintings of people in other kinds of Islamic art. In the 1500s, Muslim rulers employed artists to paint detailed pictures showing life in the royal courts and palaces. Pictures that told stories were also popular.

A busy scene

In this painting from Persia, you can see people doing many different things. Musicians are playing love songs to a prince. A man with a hawk stands beside an archer. Other characters are carrying cloth, or offering food and drink. Can you see a baby? Can you tell what everybody is doing? You can also see many different patterns that are typical of Islamic art. Can you see an example of Arabic writing?

The artist, Mir Sayyid Ali, has painted the decorative patterns very carefully. He has also taken a lot of trouble to paint people's clothes in great detail. But all the faces have exactly the same expression. Can you think of a reason for this?

Barbad Playing Music to Khusraw was one of a series of 14 miniature paintings by the Persian artist Mir Sayyid Ali.

Make your own Islamic pattern

Pattern making is more difficult than it looks! To start with, try copying a pattern from the border of this page. You could trace the pattern, or copy it onto graph paper.

When you have made the outlines, you can color them in. Look carefully at the colors that have been used on this page and in the main picture. Try to match these colors by mixing your own paints. Every time that a shape is repeated in your pattern, you must use the same color.

If you feel confident, you can design your own Islamic pattern. Think carefully about what colors to include and what shapes to use. Islamic artists often combined shapes from plants and flowers with squares, diamonds, rectangles, and stars.

Presenting your own work

Most of the pictures we have looked at in this book are framed and hung on walls. These frames are usually made from wood or plaster, and are often highly decorated. They may be carved, or even covered in gold. It looks very effective if you frame your own work, and there is a very simple way to do this. You need a large sheet of colored poster board and some tape, a metal-edged ruler and a craft knife. The knife needs to be extremely sharp, so make sure there is a grown-up with you when you use it.

Make a simple square frame for your first try. Take the picture that you want to frame and decide how wide the frame should be. Measure two squares the size of your finished frame.

Using tape, stick your picture in the middle of one of the squares you have cut out. Measure ½ inch (one centimeter) in from the edge all round your picture. Mark a shape this size on the other square of poster board, and cut it out, using the knife against the ruler as before. You will then have a frame.

Put this frame, colored side up, onto the board with your picture on it. Join the two pieces together with a hinge made out of tape. You have now framed your picture.

Mark the squares in pencil on the colored board. Then place your ruler with the metal edge against your pencil marks. Hold the ruler firmly with one hand. With the other hand, cut along your lines by drawing the blade of the knife against the ruler. Cut slowly and carefully. Don't use a ruler without a metal edge because you will probably cut into the ruler instead of cutting clear straight lines in the board.

Artists' biographies

A biography is the history of a person's life. These short biographies will help you to find out more about some of the artists mentioned in this book.

Giuseppe Arcimboldo (1527–1593)
Arcimboldo came from Milan, Italy. His best-known paintings are strange portraits made out of fruit, flowers, and vegetables. He painted many of these fantastic faces for the Hapsburg ruler Rudolf. About 300 years after his death a group of painters known as the Surrealists were inspired by Arcimboldo to paint ordinary objects in bizarre and peculiar ways.

Paul Gauguin (1848–1903)
The French artist Gauguin lived in Peru when he was a child. He was a successful businessman in Paris for some years and started painting as a hobby. Then, at age 33, he gave up his career, his home, and his family to spend his life painting. All through his life, Gauguin was fascinated by hot tropical places. He spent many years on the Pacific island of Tahiti, where he painted some of his boldest pictures. Gauguin's paintings are usually full of bright splashes of color and simple shapes.

Edvard Munch (1863–1944)
The Norwegian painter Edvard Munch had an important influence on the art of this century. He was the first member of a group of painters known as the Expressionists. Expressionists believed that art should express real feelings, even if the feelings were unpleasant or unhappy. This was very different from the way most people thought about art at the time Munch was painting. Munch traveled all over the world and made thousands of paintings and woodcuts. These pictures did not become popular until he was a very old man.

Rembrandt van Rijn (1606–1669)
The Dutch artist Rembrandt painted over 600 paintings during his life, and made more than 1,000 drawings and hundreds of etchings. We have a good record of how Rembrandt looked during his life, for he painted more than 70 self-portraits. He was very popular and successful when he was young, but in his old age he was sad and poor. Rembrandt is best known for his drawings and paintings of people. His other well-known pictures show stories about religion. Rembrandt also made some very realistic drawings of animals.

Auguste Renoir (1841–1919)

The French artist Renoir studied painting with several other painters who became known as the Impressionists. Renoir liked to paint lively groups of figures. He usually used the maids in his house as models. Renoir's pictures were full of sketchy patches of color and contrasts of light and shade. Because there wasn't much realistic detail in his paintings, people at the time often thought his pictures were careless and unfinished. Renoir painted more than 5,000 paintings. Even when he became crippled in old age, he continued painting by wedging brushes between his twisted fingers.

Henry Moore (1898–1986)

Henry Moore is one of Britain's best known sculptors. Moore started making a sculpture by looking at the stone or wood and deciding what shape it suggested to him. He first became famous in 1948 when he won an important international sculpture competition in Venice. His sculptures are usually large, and many can be seen outside, in parks or at entrances to buildings.

Sayyid Ali (c.1546–1600)

Sayyid Ali was a celebrated Persian painter. He is well known for his skill in painting miniature pictures. His major work was illustrating the story of the adventurer Hamza for the Indian Emperor Akbar. This story was told in 12 books containing over 1,000 illustrations. Sayyid Ali was in charge of a team of 100 painters, gilders, and bookbinders, and the work took 15 years to complete.

INDEX

The publishers would like to thank the following for permission to reproduce these works of art:

Cave Painting of Hunters; Hunting Fowl in the Marshes, from the Tomb of Nebamun; *Vertumnus* by Giuseppe Arcimboldo; *Yoruba Ritual Mask;* all by courtesy of the Ancient Art & Architecture Collection, London, UK. *Portrait of a Young Man* by Raphael, by courtesy of the Ashmolean Museum, Oxford, UK. *The Children's Afternoon at Wargemont* by Auguste Renoir, 1884, by courtesy of Bildarchiv Preussicher Kulturbesitz, Berlin, Germany. Self-portrait by Rembrandt, 1606-69, in Kenwood House, London, UK; *The Orrery* by Joseph Wright, 1743-97, in Derby Museum & Art Gallery, Derby, UK; *Sunday Afternoon on the Island of La Grande Jatte* by Georges Seurat, 1859-91, in the Art Institute of Chicago, USA; *The Scream* by Edvard Munch, 1863-1944, in the Nasjonalgalleriet, Oslo; *Tahitian Women on the Beach* by Paul Gauguin, 1848-1903, in the Musée Orsay, Paris, France; *Portrait of Henrietta Maria* by Anthony van Dyck, 1599-1641, in the Musée Crozatier, Le Puy en Velay, France; *Girl in a Red Dress* by Ammi Phillips, 1788-1865, in a private collection; *Portrait of a Young Man* by Nicholas Hilliard, 1547-1619, in the Victoria and Albert Museum, London, UK; *Children's Games* by Pieter Brueghel the Elder, c.1515-69, in the Kunsthistorisches Museum, Vienna, Austria; all by courtesy of the Bridgeman Art Library, London, UK. *Barbad Playing Music to Khusraw* (OR2265 f.77v) by Sayyid Ali, by courtesy of the British Library, London, UK. Inuit sculpture of a mother and child; *The Hunt* by Masayoshi; *King Louis Philippe Turning into a Pear in 4 Stages* by Honoré Daumier; *Hyena Mask from the Ibo Tribe;* all by courtesy of the Trustees of the British Museum, London, UK. Self-portrait by Albrecht Dürer, by courtesy of Graphische Sammlung Albertina, Vienna, Austria. *The Statue of Liberty* by courtesy of Greg Evans Photo Library, London, UK. *Recumbent Figure* by Henry Moore, by courtesy of the Henry Moore Foundation, Hertfordshire, UK. *Malaysian Shadow Puppets* by courtesy of the Horniman Museum, Forest Hill, London, UK. *Sassandra Mask from the Ivory Coast* by courtesy of the Musée de l'Homme, Paris, France. *A Maid Combing a Woman's Hair* by Edgar Degas; *Jesus Opens the Eyes of a Man Born Blind* by Duccio di Buoninsegna, by courtesy of the Trustees, the National Gallery, London, UK. *The Great Buddha* photograph by Nigel Blythe, by courtesy of Robert Harding Picture Library, London, UK. *Woman and Chrysanthemums* by Utagawa Kuniyoshi; *Girl with Apple* by Isaac Oliver, by courtesy of the Board of Trustees of the Victoria and Albert Museum, London, UK.

The publishers would like to give special thanks to staff at the Victoria & Albert Museum, London, and to Floyd Beckford and his colleagues at the British Museum, London.